ARCTIC FOXES

JESSIE ALKIRE

Checkerboard
Library

An Imprint of Abdo Publishing
abdobooks.com

ABDOBOOKS.COM

Published by Abdo Publishing, a division of ABDO, PO Box 398166, Minneapolis, Minnesota 55439. Copyright © 2019 by Abdo Consulting Group, Inc. International copyrights reserved in all countries. No part of this book may be reproduced in any form without written permission from the publisher. Checkerboard Library™ is a trademark and logo of Abdo Publishing.

Printed in the United States of America, North Mankato, Minnesota
102018
012019

THIS BOOK CONTAINS RECYCLED MATERIALS

Design and Production: Mighty Media, Inc.
Editor: Liz Salzmann
Cover Photographs: Shutterstock
Interior Photographs: Alamy, pp. 17, 27; iStockphoto, pp. 11, 14–15, 19, 21, 25, 28, 29; Shutterstock, pp. 5, 7, 9, 13, 22–23

Library of Congress Control Number: 2018949395

Publisher's Cataloging-in-Publication Data
Names: Alkire, Jessie, author.
Title: Arctic foxes / by Jessie Alkire.
Description: Minneapolis, Minnesota : Abdo Publishing, 2019 | Series: Arctic animals at risk | Includes online resources and index.
Identifiers: ISBN 9781532116940 (lib. bdg.) | ISBN 9781532159787 (ebook)
Subjects: LCSH: Arctic fox--Juvenile literature. | Foxes--Behavior--Juvenile literature. | Environmental protection--Arctic regions--Juvenile literature. | Habitat protection--Juvenile literature.
Classification: DDC 599.7764--dc23

TABLE OF CONTENTS

▶ **CHAPTER 1** **AN UNLIKELY PREDATOR**	4
▶ **CHAPTER 2** **ARCTIC FOXES AT RISK**	6
▶ **CHAPTER 3** **SPRING TO SUMMER**	8
▶ **CHAPTER 4** **BABY ARCTIC FOXES**	10
▶ **CHAPTER 5** **WINTER IN THE ARCTIC**	12
▶ **CHAPTER 6** **HUNTING IN SNOW**	16
▶ **CHAPTER 7** **THREATENED FOXES**	18
▶ **CHAPTER 8** **CLIMATE CHANGE**	20
▶ **CHAPTER 9** **IMPORTANCE OF ARCTIC FOXES**	24
▶ **CHAPTER 10** **SAVING ARCTIC FOXES**	26
ARCTIC FOX FACT SHEET	28
WHAT CAN YOU DO?	29
GLOSSARY	30
ONLINE RESOURCES	31
INDEX	32

AN UNLIKELY PREDATOR

Snow blankets the Arctic tundra. Everything is still. Suddenly, a flash of white crosses the snow-covered ground. It's an arctic fox! This furry, cat-sized fox doesn't look like a fierce predator. But it is an effective hunter and is ideally suited to survive in the Arctic chill.

The arctic fox freezes in its tracks. Small ears tilted forward, the fox stares at the snow-covered ground. The fox's remarkable sense of hearing has helped it find its prey. The fox hears the sound of a **rodent** tunneling below the snow. It is a **lemming**, the arctic fox's most common prey.

The arctic fox launches its body forward. It lands headfirst in the snow. The fox pulls its head out of the snow, a lemming trapped in its jaws. The fox digs a small hole with its furry paws and buries the dead lemming to eat later. The fox walks on, listening for its next prey.

There are several hundred thousand arctic foxes in the world.

CHAPTER 2

ARCTIC FOXES AT RISK

Arctic foxes belong to the family Canidae. This family includes foxes, dogs, and wolves. Arctic foxes are 20 to 24 inches (50 to 60 cm) long and weigh 6.5 to 21 pounds (2.9 to 9.5 kg). Some arctic foxes are gray-blue. But most have the long white fur arctic foxes are known for.

Arctic foxes live in the Arctic. Their range includes Russia, Alaska, Canada, Greenland, Scandinavia, and Iceland. But the arctic fox's **habitat** is being threatened.

To find food, arctic foxes rely on sea ice to travel in the winter. Unfortunately, sea ice is melting due to climate change. Without

WHAT IS CLIMATE CHANGE?

Climate change is periodic change in Earth's weather patterns. In recent years, scientists have observed an increase in the rate of climate change. Most scientists agree this is due to humans burning **fossil fuels**. Burning fossil fuels produces **greenhouse gases** which trap heat in Earth's atmosphere. This has led to rising global temperatures.

sea ice, arctic foxes can't cross water to hunt. This causes some foxes to starve.

Climate change causes warmer temperatures. As temperatures rise, other predators move north to colder areas. These predators eat the arctic fox's prey, and some may even hunt the arctic fox. While the arctic fox isn't considered **endangered** yet, scientists believe its numbers could be greatly reduced due to climate change.

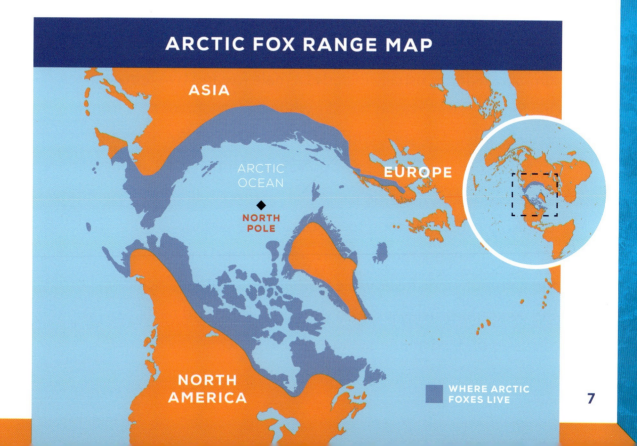

CHAPTER 3

SPRING TO SUMMER

Arctic foxes' lives are very different depending on the season. They even look different! In the spring and summer, arctic foxes have short brown or gray fur. Their fur matches the rocks and dirt around them. This helps the foxes blend in to avoid being seen by predators or prey. This shorter fur also helps arctic foxes stay cool in warmer temperatures.

Arctic foxes usually live in family groups during the spring and summer. A group usually includes a male fox and two female foxes. One female is the mating female, while the other female is from a previous litter. She stays with the family to help raise new pups.

In the summer, arctic foxes try to eat as much food as possible. This prepares them for the winter, when there is less food. Arctic foxes will also bury or hide food to eat during the winter.

Arctic foxes are mostly carnivores and tend to eat **rodents**, birds, and fish. But arctic foxes will eat whatever they can, including berries and vegetables. They will also steal eggs from bird nests, **scavenge** carcasses of dead animals, and even eat other animals' **feces**.

Some arctic foxes that live in the southern areas of their range are bluish-gray all year.

CHAPTER 4

BABY ARCTIC FOXES

Spring is also when arctic foxes mate and have babies. Each arctic fox has one mate and they often mate for life. Female arctic foxes, called vixens, give birth after 50 to 60 days. This is usually in May, June, or July.

Litter sizes can vary greatly. Some have as few as five pups, while others have up to 20! The pups are born blind with dark fur.

Arctic fox pups are born in underground dens. These dens can be very large and usually have many entrances and tunnels. Both the mother and father take care of the pups. The mother nurses the pups in the den. Meanwhile, the father hunts and brings back food.

After about three weeks, the pups venture outside the den. The pups begin hunting on their own when they are three months old. By late fall, the baby foxes are considered grown. They are ready to experience their first Arctic winter.

The size of arctic fox litters depends on food availability.

CHAPTER 5

WINTER IN THE ARCTIC

As winter begins, the arctic fox prepares for the cold months. By November, the fox's fur has grown longer and thicker. The fur has also changed to a bright white color. This helps the fox blend into the snow and ice. This way, predators such as polar bears and wolves have difficulty seeing the arctic fox in the snow.

The fox's white fur is very **insulating**. In fact, it is considered the best insulator of all land mammals. Even the soles of arctic foxes' paws are covered with fur! Body fat also helps keep arctic foxes warm. Eating extra food in the summer adds this extra layer of protection.

The arctic fox's body type is built to withstand the cold. It has a short snout, small ears, short legs, and a rounded shape. This reduces the surface area of the fox. Less surface area helps conserve heat. All these factors make the arctic fox able to survive in temperatures as cold as −65 degrees Fahrenheit (−54°C)!

During winter, arctic foxes are well camouflaged in the snow.

Unlike many other land mammals, the arctic fox doesn't **hibernate**. Instead, it travels throughout the winter. Arctic foxes roam hundreds of miles across sea ice. Arctic foxes usually spend the winters alone as they focus on survival.

If it becomes too cold to walk or if a blizzard occurs, an arctic fox will lay down and curl itself up into a small ball. It wraps its long, **bushy** tail around itself to keep warm. The fox then lets itself get completely buried in snow. The snow acts as an extra **insulator** to keep the fox warm.

 An arctic fox's tail is more than 12 inches (30 cm) long. It provides warmth and balance for the fox.

HUNTING IN SNOW

Arctic foxes' diets change considerably during the winter. Many of the animals they prey on, such as **lemmings**, burrow below the snow or even underground during winter. This makes hunting much more difficult. In one winter, an arctic fox may travel nearly 2,800 miles (4,506 km) to find food.

Arctic foxes use their keen sense of hearing to hunt prey in these conditions. Arctic foxes have wide ears that face forward. This helps them sense even the slightest sound. An arctic fox can hear a mouse or lemming moving under the snow.

Based on the prey's sound, a fox can determine the animal's exact location without seeing it! Then, the fox launches itself face-first into the snow. This helps the fox break through the snow and capture the prey in its mouth.

When arctic foxes cannot find **rodents**, they may hunt birds, such as **puffins**. Arctic foxes also follow polar bears. When a polar bear kills a seal or other animal, it may leave leftovers behind. The fox will then **scavenge** the rest of the carcass. But the fox must be sure to hide quietly in the snow. Otherwise, it could become the polar bear's next meal!

Arctic foxes eat as much as they can in the summer because prey is more plentiful then.

CHAPTER 7

THREATENED FOXES

While arctic foxes are excellent hunters themselves, they are also hunted by other predators. Both adult and baby arctic foxes can be killed by **wolverines**, red foxes, polar bears, and large birds. However, their main predator is humans.

Humans have hunted and killed arctic foxes throughout history. Many were killed for food or to protect farm animals. But arctic foxes were mostly hunted for their soft, white fur.

Arctic foxes are still trapped for their fur today. Other foxes are raised in fur farms. There, arctic foxes are bred to produce more foxes. In some cases, the pups are kept in poor conditions as they grow. When they are adults, the foxes are killed for their fur.

The desire for arctic fox fur has lessened in recent years as more people reject clothing with real animal fur. Still, hunting and fur farms have led to extreme reductions in arctic fox populations, especially in Scandinavia. Arctic fox populations in these areas have never recovered.

In the 1800s, the hide of an arctic fox could be sold for a lot of money. Just one arctic fox hide brought enough money to live on for a year!

CLIMATE CHANGE

An increasing threat to arctic foxes today is climate change. Climate change is causing temperatures to rise and sea ice to melt in the Arctic. Arctic foxes rely on the sea ice to travel in the winter and find food.

In 2008, researchers tracked the movements of 14 arctic foxes in Alaska. Eleven of the arctic foxes stayed on the mainland and did not cross sea ice. All 11 of these foxes died. Three arctic foxes crossed the sea ice throughout the winter. All three of these foxes survived.

Researchers think sea ice is very important for arctic fox survival during the winter. Not only can arctic foxes find more food as they travel, they have more room to stay away from predators. Without sea ice, arctic fox populations are expected to become smaller.

Warmer temperatures are also affecting the appearance and environment of the tundra. Bushes and trees are beginning to grow there. This area's usual mossy, rocky ground is being transformed into woodlands. Arctic foxes are not equipped for this type of habitat. They may need to move farther north to survive.

Arctic foxes that live near coasts are less affected by climate change than foxes that live inland.

The prey of arctic foxes is also affected by climate change. **Lemmings** breed and travel under the snow in the winter. However, warmer winters mean less snow. Without snow, lemmings have fewer places to burrow and breed during the winter. They are also less protected from predators. This has caused reduced lemming populations. Arctic foxes then have less prey to eat. Less food causes foxes to have fewer babies and fewer foxes to survive the winter.

Warmer temperatures and a new **tundra environment** have also caused new predators to move into arctic fox territory. The biggest threat is the red fox. Red foxes belong to the same family as arctic foxes, but they are about two times larger. They are also stronger hunters. As temperatures have risen, red foxes have moved steadily north.

When red foxes move north, they take over arctic fox territories. Red foxes eat the same prey as arctic foxes. They also take over arctic foxes' dens. Some red foxes may even hunt arctic foxes and their babies.

With reduced prey and fewer dens, arctic foxes will not be able to breed or find enough food. Some may die. Others will be forced to travel to rapidly shrinking **habitats** farther north.

 Red foxes are much more adaptable than arctic foxes. Red foxes can live in many habitats, including grasslands, mountains, and deserts.

CHAPTER 9

IMPORTANCE OF ARCTIC FOXES

To survive, arctic foxes must turn to other types of prey. These kinds of prey include young birds and eggs. This could reduce the populations of those animals. Arctic foxes may also move closer to areas where humans live in search of food. This may lead to more conflicts between humans and foxes.

Researchers have studied what would happen if the arctic fox died out. Arctic foxes are considered "ecosystem engineers." This means they greatly affect their ecosystem. One way they do this is by keeping prey populations under control. Arctic foxes are also needed as a food source for larger predators.

Arctic foxes also affect the soil in the Arctic. The soil's quality would be poor for plant growth without the help of arctic foxes. Arctic foxes spend much of the summer in dens. **Feces**, **urine**, and rotting prey from arctic foxes are left in or near dens. Many important **nutrients** from these substances soak into the soil.

This causes plants to grow where they would not otherwise. This plant life is vital for the ecosystem and is an important food source for other animals. Without arctic foxes, such plant growth would not be possible.

Many generations of arctic foxes often use the same dens. These dens can be more than one hundred years old!

SAVING ARCTIC FOXES

The fate of arctic foxes is uncertain. The International Union for the Conservation of Nature (IUCN) labels the arctic fox as Least Concern. This means the population as a whole is not **endangered**. However, arctic fox populations in Scandinavia are considered Critically Endangered.

Many organizations are working to protect arctic foxes. In 2000, the Norwegian **Environment** Agency started a program to breed arctic foxes in **captivity**. Each year, this program releases 40 to 60 foxes into the wild!

The World Wildlife Fund (WWF) also works to save arctic foxes. WWF workers bring food to areas where arctic foxes live. Some

IUCN

The International Union for the Conservation of Nature is a global authority on the **status** of wildlife. It collects scientific data and experts' studies to determine the status of a species. Then, governments and conservation organizations use this information to make decisions about species protection.

26

Some arctic foxes are tagged. This helps researchers track and monitor the foxes over time.

groups work to control or move red foxes out of arctic fox territories. These efforts have increased arctic fox populations in Sweden.

Organizations such as WWF and Defenders of Wildlife work to raise awareness about climate change. These organizations also support laws to reduce **greenhouse gas** emissions. With breeding programs, raised awareness, and new laws, real change can occur to save the arctic fox!

ARCTIC FOX FACT SHEET

SCIENTIFIC NAME: *Vulpes lagopus*

LENGTH: 20 to 24 inches (50 to 60 cm)

WEIGHT: 6.5 to 21 pounds (2.9 to 9.5 kg)

DIET: omnivore

AVERAGE LIFESPAN IN THE WILD: 3 to 6 years

IUCN STATUS: Least Concern

WHAT CAN YOU DO?

You can take action to help arctic foxes and other Arctic animals at risk!

▶ Give money to or volunteer for arctic fox conservation organizations. These include World Wildlife Fund, Defenders of Wildlife, and the Arctic Fox Centre.

▶ Write to local lawmakers asking them to support policies that protect arctic foxes. These policies include laws that limit **greenhouse gas** emissions.

▶ Tell your friends and family about climate change and how it affects Arctic wildlife such as arctic foxes.

▶ Reduce your individual use of **fossil fuels** by choosing to bike, walk, or take the bus instead of riding in a car.

GLOSSARY

bushy—very thick and full.

captivity—the state of living in a prison or a cage instead of in the wild.

endangered—in danger of becoming extinct.

environment—all the surroundings that affect the growth and well-being of a living thing.

feces—solid bodily waste.

fossil fuel—a fuel formed in the earth from the remains of plants or animals. Coal, oil, and natural gas are fossil fuels.

greenhouse gas—a gas, such as carbon dioxide, that traps heat in Earth's atmosphere.

habitat—a place where a living thing is naturally found.

hibernate—to spend a period of time, such as the winter, in deep sleep.

insulate—to keep something from losing heat. Something that prevents a loss of heat is an insulator.

lemming—a small rodent that lives in northern areas of North America, Europe, and Asia.

nutrient—a substance that plants, animals, and people need to live and grow.

puffin—a seabird that lives in the north Atlantic and is black-and-white with a colorful bill.

rodent—any of several related animals that have large front teeth for gnawing. Common rodents include mice, squirrels, and lemmings.

scavenge—to search through waste for something that can be used.

status—a state or a condition.

tundra—cold, dry, treeless land in the Arctic. Below the surface, the ground is permanently frozen.

urine—waste material produced by the kidneys. In mammals, urine is usually a yellowish liquid.

wolverine—a North American animal with brown shaggy fur that looks like a small bear but is related to the weasel.

ONLINE RESOURCES

To learn more about arctic foxes, visit **abdobooklinks.com**. These links are routinely monitored and updated to provide the most current information available.

INDEX

A
Alaska, 6, 20

B
babies, 10, 18, 21, 23
body type, 12

C
camouflage, 8, 12
Canada, 6
climate change, 6, 7, 20, 21, 23, 27
conservation efforts, 26, 27

D
dens, 10, 23, 24
diet, 4, 8, 16, 17, 21, 24

E
ears, 4, 12, 16
effect on ecosystem, 24, 25

F
family groups, 8
fox hunting, 18
fur, 6, 8, 10, 12, 18

G
Greenland, 6

H
habitat, 6, 20, 23
humans, 18, 24
hunting, 4, 6, 7, 8, 10, 16, 20, 23

I
Iceland, 6
International Union for the Conservation of Nature, 26

L
lemmings, 4, 16, 21

M
mating, 8, 10

N
Norwegian Environment Agency, 26

P
polar bears, 12, 16, 17, 18
population decline, 7, 18, 20, 21, 23
predators, 7, 8, 12, 17, 18, 20, 23, 24

R
range, 6, 7, 20
red foxes, 18, 23, 27
research, 20, 24, 26

S
Scandinavia, 6, 18, 26
sea ice, 6, 7, 15, 20
size, 4, 6, 23
spring, 8, 10
summer, 8, 12, 24
Sweden, 26, 27

T
tail, 15
threats, 6, 7, 18, 20, 23
traveling, 6, 7, 15, 16, 20
tundra, 4, 20, 23

W
winter, 4, 6, 8, 10, 12, 15, 16, 20, 21
World Wildlife Fund, 26, 27